D0580004

Thank you for 25 years

To:

From:

Brian

SH*T

I WISH I KNEW

25 Lessons Over 25 Years

©2019 by Renie Cavallari International, LLC. All rights reserved. No part of this publication may be reproduced in any form or by any means without the written permission of the author.

Design by Cortney Tucker.

To contact Renie Cavallari,
email renie@poweredbyaspire.com.

Visit poweredbyaspire.com.

RCI Publishing

ISBN: 978-0-9906992-0-0

Printed in the U.S.A.

INSPIRE.DISЯUPT.ALIGN.

Thank you...

for 25 years of inspiration, patience and collaboration. It is hard to believe that 25 years ago we started on this journey. For many of you, it's been all 25 years – and to all of you, I am so grateful.

Thank you for believing in us. For sharing your hopes and fears. For the laughter and the tears. For the collaboration and extraordinary impact we have accomplished together. You have stretched us, and we are better for it.

What an incredible ride it has been. A labor of love.

Thank you to the global aspire team. Thank you to Barbara for 22 years and JC for leading us into the future. Thank you to everyone who is and has been a team member. Thank you for all of your hard work and commitment in living our promise everyday: to awaken the potential and ignite the shine in those we get to hang with every day.

And lastly, thank you to my family. My mother, the believer. My sister, Meg, the cheerleader. My brother, Seth, the perspective. And to my daughter, Bella, the inspiration of my life. Thank you all for enhancing my world.

Here's to the next 25 years of awakening and to the shit I wish I knew.

Love, Renie

It's always about your people.

I have worked with so many fantastic people over the years. Team members. Clients. Partners. Alliances. What I do know is that humans are complex and at the same time simple. We all need connection. We all need people who believe in us. We all need a sense of belonging and the certainty that our contributions are valued. What I have come to know is that when you give people what they need they play all in. Thank god for people!

Small shit actually matters.

They say don't sweat the small stuff and in my experience it's the small stuff that makes a big difference. Start each day with "what matters most" and move with that intention in mind.

What you focus on comes true!

Build a
career that
serves your life.

Not a life
that serves
your career.

Over the years so many people gave me "advice". You have to grow bigger. Their definition of success was how many "FTEs" we had. The paradigm that bigger is better or safer is bullshit. Build something that has a purpose, a heart and soul, and that contributes. Build something that touches lives. Build something that allows you to have a life.

Case in point: I cooked dinner for my daughter, Bella, every night we were together. My workday was over at 6pm so we had quality time. That didn't mean I didn't work after she went to bed, but it did mean I was going to be present for those precious hours we had together. It is the relationships of my life that have always mattered to me.

Whether you own the company or work for a great company is immaterial. Be a part of something that makes a difference and that enhances your life.

Lead with compassion balanced with accountability.

Leading with compassion and love has been critical to aspire's success. As a company, we are always hired to disrupt the status quo and improve performance, which is code for: changing and improving competencies and results. When you deal with change for a living, compassion is a good place to start.

The real challenge for me over the years has been to learn to balance compassion with accountability. When I didn't, I inadvertently created enabling environments and that's the worst kind of leadership. When you enable people, even when it is with the best of intentions, you disempower them. Without 100% responsibility there is no accountability.

As they say, the road to hell is paved with good intentions!

Inspect what you expect or don't expect much.

When you don't like what you are seeing, step back and consider – how did you set up the expectations. The 3 greatest accountability questions are:
- What will you do?
- By when will you do it?
- How will I know?

It's the "how I will know" that can be the trick. Lack of follow through creates a culture that lacks accountability. This doesn't mean you chase people for the status. It means they follow up with you on their commitments.

When I hear leaders say, "Well, I can't count on them..." I ask, "How often do you inspect what you expect?" You only have to do it a few times and people come to know..."live to your commitments" as that feeling of dropping the ball feels like shit to everyone.

Words are cheap. If you want results, set expectations and inspect what you expect.

Balance is Bullshit.

You are always out of balance.

Some days family is first.

Other days, and nights for that matter, it's work. Own it.

Embrace the reality that everyday has a different imbalance. I can't tell you how many years I spent feeling bad after putting balance on my new year's resolutions list!

It isn't balance you long for – its joy.

How you get your joy is your choice.

Listen more. Talk less.

If you want to understand people and their perspectives, the 80-20 rule works best. If you don't believe me, ask Oprah, the greatest talk show host of all times. Watch her...she asks great questions, connects deeply, and only speaks 20% of the time. Brilliant!

People have drama.

Stop hoping they won't.

It's a package deal.

Be humble or get ready to be humbled.

I want to apologize to all those I negatively impacted when I was certain I knew everything there was to know. When my listening shut down. When I didn't have the courage to be vulnerable or lacked the depth of character to be self-aware. When I reflect back on when I was at my worst, it was always because I lacked the humility to see what was in front of me, coupled with the arrogance to think I could somehow control everything. I'm sure I gave God many a good laugh!

In my experience, humility improves with age... like a fine wine.

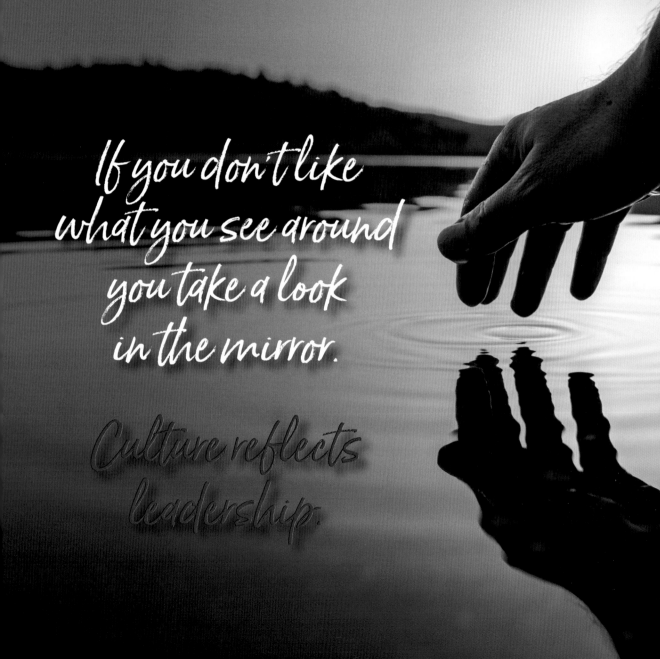

If you don't like what you see around you take a look in the mirror.

Culture reflects leadership.

In 25 years aspire's culture has slipped more than once. The pattern I've identified is consistent. Ever so quietly, the pot stirrers would commandeer our culture. I always made the same mistake: being allergic to negativity, I would distance myself versus challenge it the moment I saw it.

Culture is like our own physical health. Whether it's being taken care of properly is up to you.

In the end, culture reflects leadership... and leadership is a behavior not a position.

Who you hang with is who you become.

Our life is impacted by our environment. And our environment is a derivative of the people we are surrounded by. People are either enhancing your world or depleting it. Unfortunately, sometimes you have to make the tough decision to fire the "depleters".

Take a close look around.
A very close look.

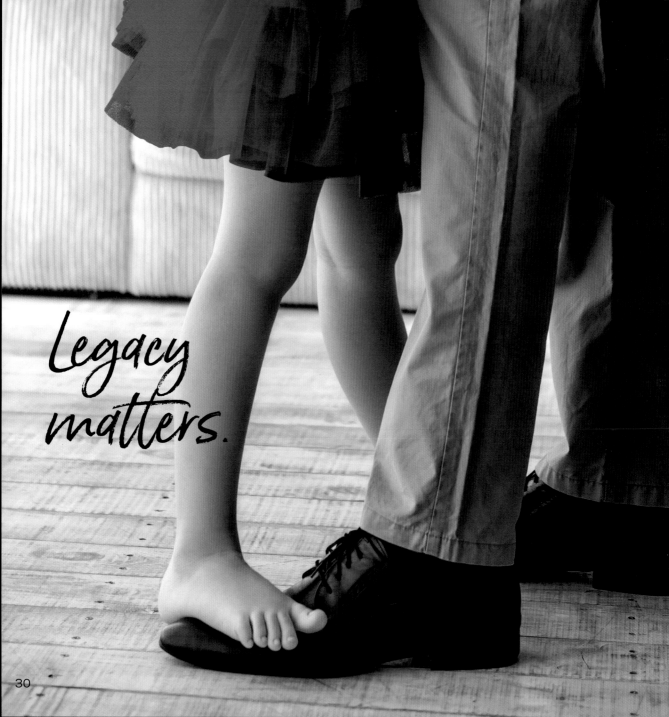

Legacy
matters.

As my father used to say,

"In life you have to bring your good time with you."

Words to live by!

His legacy fueled my courage to live life differently, and always my way. What a ride I am having!

Thank you, Daddy.

Miss you daily!

You're just not everyone's flavor.

Stop wasting time worrying about what other people think of you. You can't control other people's perceptions.

Most of my career, people would say "you are so strong, so driven, so powerful...", implying it was some kind of character flaw. It always made me feel bad and made me question if I should *play smaller*.

My Kool Aid Formula:

- Know who you are and what you value.
- Work on the shit that limits your potential.
- Always be the best version of your true self.
- Play all in.
- And accept, "I'm just not everyone's flavor!".

People come and go.

Being an employer for 25 years has had its ups and downs. I hate losing talented people and have had to come to peace that their choice was personal... to them.

Inevitably, they needed something that we could not provide. I am so grateful that I remain connected to most of them and am so proud of how they have thrived.

I believe that the real challenge is helping people leave without feeling a need to blame and shame. The real opportunity is to respect each other as we go "our separate ways".

I still hate losing talented people, but I have come to know it's an opportunity for everyone to learn, grow and succeed at a higher level.

HeadTrash
is the leading killer
of potential.

You know those voices.

The little people in our brain that, when acting out, can wreak havoc and promote negativity against ourselves!

We cannot change our life's experiences and they can produce some stinky trash.
Be aware of its impact on you and dump it!

It doesn't serve you and you were born to serve the world.

For the love of serving

People either thrive in serving others or they don't. If you watch closely, they will tell you which side of the "In service to others" fence they are on. I have wasted far too many hours hoping that people will come around. What I have come to know is that people either have it or they don't.

Fire the Pukers.

The Blamers. The Shamers. The C.A.V.E. (Constantly Against Virtually Everything) People. Making others wrong doesn't serve anyone. Own every problem and you move to solution quickly. Excuses are boring. Pukers are the cancer of any organization. Fire them as they are not interested in making things better. They suck the air out of everyone and are a mental and physical health risk.

P.S. Puker Fact: We are all pukers at times, and it is when we settle into negativity that it is time to make a change in our mind set. Nothing positive comes from negativity.

When your
gut says no,
go with NO!

Your gut is your knowledge, instincts and observations all coming together to tell you something. My biggest mistakes have always been the ones where I had the information to make a smarter decision and didn't have the courage to listen.

So annoying!

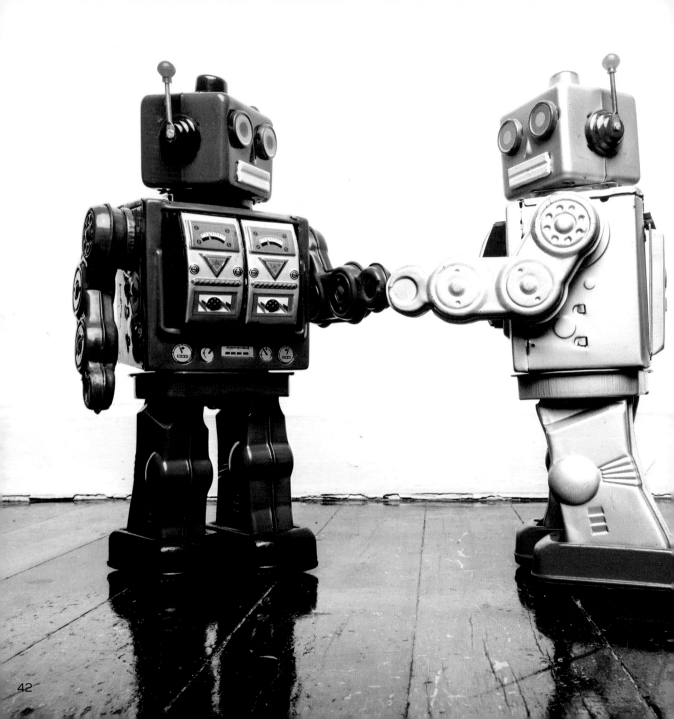

A bad hire
is a bad hire.

Take the hit

and move on.

Stop hoping you

are wrong.

You aren't.

Embrace change
as you either lead
it or it leads you.

Shit changes!

Self-awareness is one of life's most underrated skills.

Every experience, no matter how
fantastic or painful at the time,
has value if you choose to reflect on it.
The more self-aware you are, the more
you evolve and open yourself up to
your true potential.

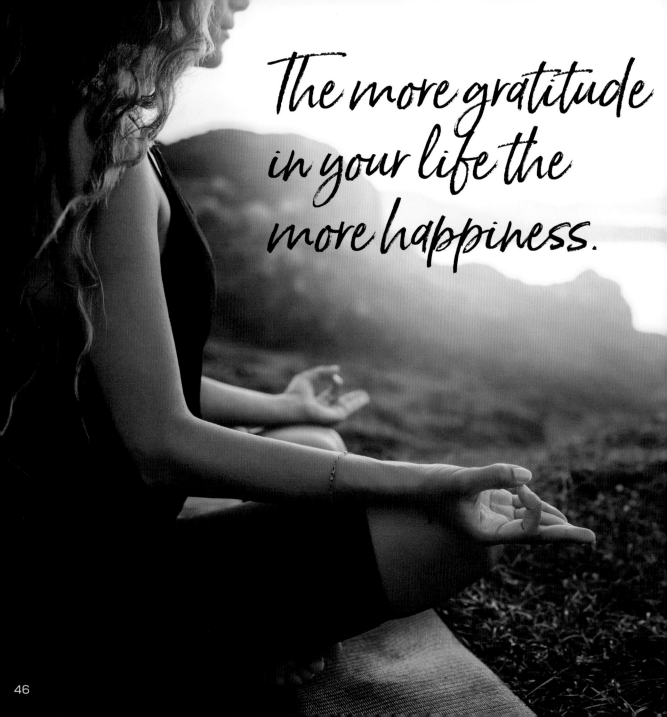

The more gratitude in your life the more happiness.

Focus on gratitude.

It sets the tempo of your
day and fills your life with
appreciation and joy.
Start with gratitude every
morning...and end there
every night.

Passion is the fuel of your life.

Passion is the combustion of energy, emotion and focus coming together to power your soul. Live with passion and you get to live an extraordinary fulfilling life.

Be an
innovator.

It's more interesting.

It's more fun.

It's more rewarding

as few people dare to

color outside the lines.

It's important work.

#thinkdifferent #bebold

Align to Thrive.

Team alignment is the greatest predictor of organizational success. Everyone leads regardless of their position, as leadership is a behavior not a position.

Alignment comes from living the 6 Pillars of Intentional Leadership:

1. Connection
2. Clean Communication
3. Compassion
4. Higher Purpose
5. Participation/Engagement
6. 100% Responsibility/Accountability

Love

We are obsessed with love.

Love for our craft. Love for those we get to hang with.
Love for the haters and the lovers.

We have a love for disrupting the status quo,
for kick ass results and a crazy love for learning.

To be in love is to be alive.

And then there is our love of leading.
Leading ourselves. Leading our industry.

We are the believers.
We believe in people.

Shit that
didn't make
the top 25

Real conversations are not always easy ones to have.

If you want to be a great leader, you have to have the courage to have them.

Stop hoping that others will make you happy.

Your happiness is a reflection of your choices. If you don't like where your life is, make a new choice. Choose wisely.

I wish I worried less.

It's such a useless drain of energy.

Why haven't they made a pill for that?!

Be kind.

It's free. It's a choice. It changes another person's day.

"Kindness Changes Everything".

Check out the be kind people project: www.bkpp.org. They are changing the world through our greatest resource...our children.

aspire

INSPIRE.DISЯUPT.ALIGN.

poweredbyaspire.com